This Fucking Planner Belongs to:

T0322324

we're getting
fucking
married

sourcebooks

Contents

Planning Your Wedding Should Be a Piece of Fucking Cake...

Congrats! You're getting fucking married!

Now it's time for the fun part—planning! If you raised an eyebrow at *planning* and *fun*, this planner is going to prove you wrong. Filled with details and tips and tricks for preparing for your big day, this wedding planner has all the necessary essentials you need to make the planning process is a piece of fucking cake. Oh, and there are hilarious swears to help you laugh off the stress and remember that this really is fucking fun!

To make shit even simpler, we've included all the basics and where to find them in the table of contents for your convenience!

Important Shit to Remember

Name & Title:	
PHONE	EMAIL

Name & Title:	
PHONE	EMAIL

Name & Title:	
PHONE	EMAIL

Name & Title:

PHONE	EMAIL

Name & Title:

PHONE	EMAIL

Name & Title:

PHONE	EMAIL

Name & Title:

PHONE	EMAIL

Name & Title:

PHONE	EMAIL

Name & Title:

PHONE	EMAIL

Name & Title:

PHONE	EMAIL

Name & Title:

PHONE	EMAIL

Name & Title:

PHONE	EMAIL

Name & Title:

PHONE	EMAIL

Name & Title:

PHONE	EMAIL

Name & Title:

PHONE	EMAIL

Name & Title:

PHONE	EMAIL

Name & Title:

PHONE	EMAIL

Name & Title:

PHONE	EMAIL

Name & Title:

PHONE	EMAIL

Name & Title:

PHONE	EMAIL

Name & Title:

PHONE	EMAIL

Name & Title:

PHONE	EMAIL

Name & Title:

PHONE	EMAIL

Name & Title:

PHONE	EMAIL

Name & Title:	
PHONE	EMAIL

Name & Title:	
PHONE	EMAIL

Name & Title:	
PHONE	EMAIL

Name & Title:	
PHONE	EMAIL

Name & Title:	
PHONE	EMAIL

Name & Title:	
PHONE	EMAIL

Name & Title:	
PHONE	EMAIL

Name & Title:

PHONE	EMAIL

Name & Title:

PHONE	EMAIL

Name & Title:

PHONE	EMAIL

Name & Title:

PHONE	EMAIL

Name & Title:

PHONE	EMAIL

Name & Title:

PHONE	EMAIL

Name & Title:

PHONE	EMAIL

The Big Fucking Picture

Planning a wedding is a fucking marathon, so start getting your shit together early so that all of your to-dos are checked off by the wedding date. This checklist is a damn good place to start!

12+ MONTHS BEFORE

☐ Time to crunch some damn numbers and create your wedding budget (see page 30 for help on this shit.)

☐ Start thinking about what you want your wedding to look like (check out page 18 to get the ideas rolling).

☐ Begin researching and touring ceremony and reception venues.

☐ _____

_____

☐ _____

_____

☐ _____

_____

☐ _____

_____

9–11 MONTHS BEFORE

- [ ] Recruit your best bitches for your bridal or wedding party.
- [ ] Set a date and time.
- [ ] Book your venues and nonnegotiable vendors.
- [ ] Finalize the whole damn guest list.
- [ ] Shop till you fucking drop for wedding day attire.
- [ ] Take some damn time to make a wedding registry.
- [ ] _____

  _____
- [ ] _____

  _____
- [ ] _____

  _____

7–8 MONTHS BEFORE

- [ ] Send out save-the-dates.
- [ ] Secure any wedding insurance policies...because shit happens.
- [ ] Get your rehearsal dinner venue on the books.
- [ ] Start researching and making reservations for your honeymoon.
- [ ] _____

  _____
- [ ] _____

  _____
- [ ] _____

  _____

5–6 MONTHS BEFORE

- [ ] Go ring shopping!
- [ ] Book your glam squad (aka hair and makeup team), if using.
- [ ] Order formal invites.
- [ ] Figure out the fucking menu.
- [ ] Book an officiant for the ceremony.
- [ ] Select final bouquet and boutonniere styles.
- [ ] Finish getting all honeymoon plans and shit together.
- [ ] _____
  _____
- [ ] _____
  _____
- [ ] _____
  _____

3–4 MONTHS BEFORE

- [ ] Finalize the ceremony schedule.
- [ ] Send bridal shower invites.
- [ ] Throw your bridal or wedding shower!
- [ ] Send formal wedding invites.
- [ ] Start brainstorming a music wish-list.
- [ ] _____
  _____
- [ ] _____
  _____

2 MONTHS BEFORE

- ☐ Sit the fuck down and write your vows.
- ☐ Purchase gifts for your fucking awesome wedding party.
- ☐ Pick a first-dance song and songs for dances with the parents.
- ☐ Start gathering items for welcome bags and party favors.
- ☐ _____
  _____
- ☐ _____
  _____
- ☐ _____
  _____
- ☐ _____
  _____

1 MONTH BEFORE

- ☐ Apply for a marriage license—you're getting fucking married!
- ☐ Someone has to plan that damn seating chart.
- ☐ Confirm the wedding party's attire.
- ☐ _____
  _____
- ☐ _____
  _____
- ☐ _____
  _____
- ☐ _____

2 WEEKS BEFORE

☐ Review and confirm RSVPs.

☐ Make a list of all the angles and shots you definitely fucking want and send it to your photographer.

☐ Touch base and confirm any last-minute details with the vendors.

☐ Make sure you have all final beauty appointments booked and ready.

☐ Pass along music requests to your DJ.

☐ Polish up those vows.

☐ Finalize the seating plan and make place cards.

☐ _____

_____

☐ _____

_____

☐ _____

_____

☐ _____

_____

☐ _____

_____

☐ _____

_____

☐ _____

THE WEEK OF...

- [ ] Practice reading your vows aloud.

- [ ] Give your venue and caterer the final headcount.

- [ ] Confirm the timing with all your vendors.

- [ ] Get your wedding day attire steamed and pressed.

- [ ] Do your final fitting, and try on your attire with those cute-ass shoes!

- [ ] Pack for the honeymoon.

- [ ] Start writing thank-you notes.

- [ ] Whoo! You made it to the rehearsal dinner.

- [ ] _____

  _____

- [ ] _____

  _____

- [ ] _____

  _____

- [ ] _____

  _____

- [ ] _____

  _____

- [ ] _____

  _____

- [ ] _____

SHIT, IT'S THE WEDDING DAY

- [ ] Relax and have fun, bitch!

Dream Big, Damn It

Do you keep hearing all this stuff about your "wedding vision" but have no fucking idea what that is? Or maybe your Pinterest board is packed with so much wedding inspo shit that it's hard to narrow down what you want? These questions are here to help you block out all that external clutter and figure out what fuck *you* want in your dream wedding.

What are your biggest priorities? Do you want to splash some cash on the venue or do you want to make sure you can accommodate a lot of guests? What's more important, flowers or food?

What is the ultimate goal for your wedding? What do you want to get out of your big day?

What is the feeling and personality of your dream wedding?

Is tradition important for you or for your families? Are there any traditions that you want to incorporate, or do you want to do your own thing?

In three words, what will your wedding be (e.g., traditional, intimate, modern, cultural, elegant, romantic, whimsical, fucking amazing, big-ass party, etc.)?

Wedding of My Fucking Dreams

Paste in all your damn inspiration photos here!

My Fucking Wedding Vision

With so many options out there, identifying what you want for your wedding can be *really fucking hard*. Use these next few pages to guide your thinking and help you make decisions throughout the planning process. And if you're feeling overwhelmed at any point in the planning process, this is here for you to flip back to and remember your damn beautiful wedding vision!

Circle the items and features that you'd like to include, and put a big-ass star next to the things you must have!

TYPE OF WEDDING

Large guest list (more than 100 guests)	Small guest list (less than 100 guests)	Destination wedding	Religious ceremony	Rehearsal dinner
Outdoors	Indoors	Daytime wedding	Evening wedding	Day-after brunch

COLORS

Green	Blue	Violet	Blush pink	Yellow
Red	Black	Earth tones	_____	_____
_____	_____	_____	_____	_____

CEREMONY

Standard vows	Self-written vows	Special readings	Family and/or friend officiant	Religious officiant
Flower girls	Ring bearer	Bridal party	Live music	Playlist

RECEPTION

Champagne toast	Open bar	Full-service meal
Buffet meal	Dance floor	DJ
Games and/or karaoke	Receiving line	First dance
Dances with the parents	Garter toss	Bouquet toss
Toasts	Cake cutting	Grand exit
Getaway car	Limo	

OTHER

Wedding planner	Photographer and/or videographer	Caterer	Hair and makeup team	Musicians
_____	_____	_____	_____	_____

ANOTHER FUCKING TIP: Selecting your top five priorities out of everything you circled is helpful when deciding what is worth splurging on and what you could DIY.

WEDDING ATTIRE

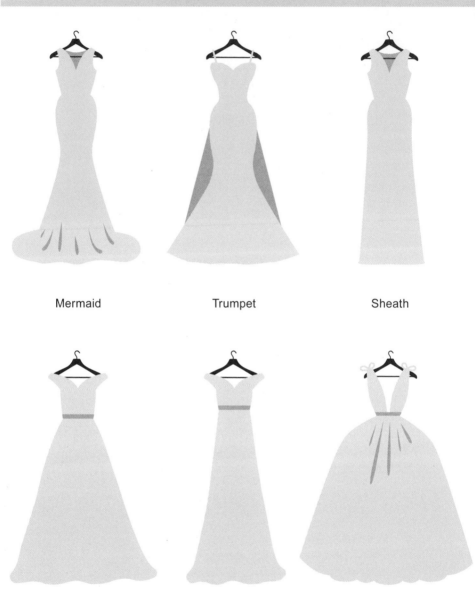

Mermaid

Trumpet

Sheath

A-Line

Empire

Ball Gown

Column

Tea-Length

Peak

Wide Peak

Narrow Notch

Standard Notch

Wide Notch

Shawl

Something Else

Something Else

My Fucking Wedding Budget

Don't skip this part—it's important to sit your ass down and crunch some numbers before planning. There are three big considerations to think about when figuring out how much you can, and are willing, to spend: your personal savings, contributions from the parents, and day-to-day bills (these motherfucking bills don't disappear just because you're getting married).

Use this worksheet to organize your budget by category. Each budget space has extra room for you to personalize and add items that are unique to your wedding! Check out the tips throughout for ideas of what else may need to be included in your wedding budget.

WHAT ELSE GOES HERE? If you are spending money on undergarments, jewelry, hair, makeup, nails, or anything else, include those expenses in this table.

Attire: Partner One

	BUDGETED COST	ACTUAL COST
Outfit		
Alterations		
Shoes		
Makeup		
Hair		
Total		

Attire: Partner Two

	BUDGETED COST	ACTUAL COST
Outfit		
Alterations		
Shoes		
Makeup		
Hair		
Total		

Ceremony

	BUDGETED COST	ACTUAL COST
Ceremony Site		
Officiant		
Rental Fees		
Total		

WHAT ELSE GOES HERE? If you are spending money on decor, flower arrangements, live music, or anything else, include those expenses in this table.

Reception

	BUDGETED COST	ACTUAL COST
Venue		
Total		

WHAT ELSE GOES HERE? If you are paying any additional reception fees on things like parking, coat check, or gratuities, include those expenses here.

Food & Drink

	BUDGETED COST	ACTUAL COST
Food		
Bar		
Dessert		
Service		
Total		

Stationery

	BUDGETED COST	ACTUAL COST
Invitations		
Response Cards		
Place Cards		
Total		

WHAT ELSE GOES HERE? If you plan to purchase programs, thank-you cards, save-the-date announcements, or any type of stationery for your wedding, include those expenses in this table.

Flowers

	BUDGETED COST	ACTUAL COST
Ceremony		
Bride's Bouquet		
Bridesmaids' Bouquets		
Centerpieces		
Total		

WHAT ELSE GOES HERE? If you want to spend money on boutonnieres, corsages, or on extra floral decorations, include those expenses here.

Music

	BUDGETED COST	ACTUAL COST
Ceremony		
Reception		
Total		

Parties		
	BUDGETED COST	ACTUAL COST
Bridal Shower		
Rehearsal Dinner		
Total		

WHAT ELSE GOES HERE? If you are having an engagement party, post-wedding brunch, bachelorette party, bachelor party, or bach party, budget for those expenses here.

Photography		
	BUDGETED COST	ACTUAL COST
Photographer		
Videographer		
Wedding Portraits		
Total		

WHAT ELSE GOES HERE? If you want to spend money on engagement portraits or wedding albums, include those expenses here.

Transportation

	BUDGETED COST	ACTUAL COST
Airfare		
Hotel		
Total		

WHAT ELSE GOES HERE? If you are using any ride-share services, cabs, buses, trains, or fucking fancy limousines, budget for those expenses here.

Miscellaneous Expenses

	BUDGETED COST	ACTUAL COST
Total		

Total Wedding Expenses

	BUDGETED COST	ACTUAL COST
Total		

Fucking Headcount

Determining your guest list is one of the most important tasks on the wedding planning checklist. The size of your guest list will affect your venue, budget, and many other aspects of your wedding day.

ANOTHER FUCKING TIP: Does your guest have a dietary requirement, a plus one, or need disability accessible seating? Record all those details here so you can remember them while planning.

Name:	
RSVP	ADDITIONAL INFO
Y / N	

Name:	
RSVP	ADDITIONAL INFO
Y / N	

Name:	
RSVP	ADDITIONAL INFO
Y / N	

Name:	
RSVP	ADDITIONAL INFO
Y / N	

Name:	
RSVP	ADDITIONAL INFO
Y / N	

Name:	
RSVP	ADDITIONAL INFO
Y / N	

Name:	
RSVP	ADDITIONAL INFO
Y / N	

Name:	
RSVP	ADDITIONAL INFO
Y / N	

Name:	
RSVP	ADDITIONAL INFO
Y / N	

Name:	
RSVP	ADDITIONAL INFO
Y / N	

Name:	
RSVP	ADDITIONAL INFO
Y / N	

Name:	
RSVP	ADDITIONAL INFO
Y / N	

Name:	
RSVP	ADDITIONAL INFO
Y / N	

Name:	
RSVP	ADDITIONAL INFO
Y / N	

Name:	
RSVP	ADDITIONAL INFO
Y / N	

Name:	
RSVP	ADDITIONAL INFO
Y / N	

Name:	
RSVP	ADDITIONAL INFO
Y / N	

Name:	
RSVP	ADDITIONAL INFO
Y / N	

Name:	
RSVP	ADDITIONAL INFO
Y / N	

Name:	
RSVP	ADDITIONAL INFO
Y / N	

Name:	
RSVP	ADDITIONAL INFO
Y / N	

Name:	
RSVP	ADDITIONAL INFO
Y / N	

Name:	
RSVP	ADDITIONAL INFO
Y / N	

Name:	
RSVP	ADDITIONAL INFO
Y / N	

Name:	
RSVP	ADDITIONAL INFO
Y / N	

Name:	
RSVP	ADDITIONAL INFO
Y / N	

Name:	
RSVP	ADDITIONAL INFO
Y / N	

Name:	
RSVP	ADDITIONAL INFO
Y / N	

Name:	
RSVP	ADDITIONAL INFO
Y / N	

Name:	
RSVP	ADDITIONAL INFO
Y / N	

Name:	
RSVP	ADDITIONAL INFO
Y / N	

Name:	
RSVP	ADDITIONAL INFO
Y / N	

Name:	
RSVP	ADDITIONAL INFO
Y / N	

Name:	
RSVP	ADDITIONAL INFO
Y / N	

Name:	
RSVP	ADDITIONAL INFO
Y / N	

Name:	
RSVP	ADDITIONAL INFO
Y / N	

Name:	
RSVP	ADDITIONAL INFO
Y / N	

Name:	
RSVP	ADDITIONAL INFO
Y / N	

Name:	
RSVP	ADDITIONAL INFO
Y / N	

Name:	
RSVP	ADDITIONAL INFO
Y / N	

Name:	
RSVP	ADDITIONAL INFO
Y / N	

Name:	
RSVP	ADDITIONAL INFO
Y / N	

Name:	
RSVP	ADDITIONAL INFO
Y / N	

Name:	
RSVP	ADDITIONAL INFO
Y / N	

Name:	
RSVP	ADDITIONAL INFO
Y / N	

Name:	
RSVP	ADDITIONAL INFO
Y / N	

Name:	
RSVP	ADDITIONAL INFO
Y / N	

Name:	
RSVP	ADDITIONAL INFO
Y / N	

Name:	
RSVP	ADDITIONAL INFO
Y / N	

Name:	
RSVP	ADDITIONAL INFO
Y / N	

Name:	
RSVP	ADDITIONAL INFO
Y / N	

Name:	
RSVP	ADDITIONAL INFO
Y / N	

Name:	
RSVP	ADDITIONAL INFO
Y / N	

Name:	
RSVP	ADDITIONAL INFO
Y / N	

Name:	
RSVP	ADDITIONAL INFO
Y / N	

Name:	
RSVP	ADDITIONAL INFO
Y / N	

Name:	
RSVP	ADDITIONAL INFO
Y / N	

Name:	
RSVP	ADDITIONAL INFO
Y / N	

Name:	
RSVP	ADDITIONAL INFO
Y / N	

Name:	
RSVP	ADDITIONAL INFO
Y / N	

Name:	
RSVP	ADDITIONAL INFO
Y / N	

Name:	
RSVP	ADDITIONAL INFO
Y / N	

Name:	
RSVP	ADDITIONAL INFO
Y / N	

Name:	
RSVP	ADDITIONAL INFO
Y / N	

Name:	
RSVP	ADDITIONAL INFO
Y / N	

Name:	
RSVP	ADDITIONAL INFO
Y / N	

Name:	
RSVP	ADDITIONAL INFO
Y / N	

Name:	
RSVP	ADDITIONAL INFO
Y / N	

Name:	
RSVP	ADDITIONAL INFO
Y / N	

Name:	
RSVP	ADDITIONAL INFO
Y / N	

Name:	
RSVP	ADDITIONAL INFO
Y / N	

Name:	
RSVP	ADDITIONAL INFO
Y / N	

Name:	
RSVP	ADDITIONAL INFO
Y / N	

Name:	
RSVP	ADDITIONAL INFO
Y / N	

Name:	
RSVP	ADDITIONAL INFO
Y / N	

Name:	
RSVP	ADDITIONAL INFO
Y / N	

Name:	
RSVP	ADDITIONAL INFO
Y / N	

Name:	
RSVP	ADDITIONAL INFO
Y / N	

Name:	
RSVP	ADDITIONAL INFO
Y / N	

Name:	
RSVP	ADDITIONAL INFO
Y / N	

Name:	
RSVP	ADDITIONAL INFO
Y / N	

Name:	
RSVP	ADDITIONAL INFO
Y / N	

Name:	
RSVP	ADDITIONAL INFO
Y / N	

Name:	
RSVP	ADDITIONAL INFO
Y / N	

Name:	
RSVP	ADDITIONAL INFO
Y / N	

Name:	
RSVP	ADDITIONAL INFO
Y / N	

Name:	
RSVP	ADDITIONAL INFO
Y / N	

Name:	
RSVP	ADDITIONAL INFO
Y / N	

The Party Awaits, Bitches

The ceremony and reception are often just one of many parties that a couple will throw. Whether you're planning an engagement party, rehearsal dinner, day-after brunch, bridal shower, bachelorette party, or some other sort of celebratory shit, planning these extra events can be a lot of fucking work.

These pages are here to help you to get your shit together and organize the never-ending details that come with planning your wedding parties. So, grab a pen. It's time to fucking plan.

What party are you throwing?

VENUE	
LOCATION	
HOST	
DATE/TIME	

	FOOD AND DRINKS	Y / N

Menu

APPETIZERS	
ENTRÉES	
DESSERTS	
BEVERAGES	

Additional Information:

What party are you throwing?

VENUE	
LOCATION	
HOST	
DATE/TIME	**FOOD AND DRINKS** Y / N

Menu

APPETIZERS	
ENTRÉES	
DESSERTS	
BEVERAGES	

Additional Information:

What party are you throwing?

VENUE	
LOCATION	
HOST	
DATE/TIME	

	FOOD AND DRINKS	Y / N

Menu

APPETIZERS	
ENTRÉES	
DESSERTS	
BEVERAGES	

Additional Information:

What party are you throwing?

VENUE	
LOCATION	
HOST	
DATE/TIME	

		FOOD AND DRINKS	Y / N

Menu

APPETIZERS	
ENTRÉES	
DESSERTS	
BEVERAGES	

Additional Information:

What party are you throwing?

VENUE	
LOCATION	
HOST	
DATE/TIME		FOOD AND DRINKS	Y / N

Menu

APPETIZERS	
ENTRÉES	
DESSERTS	
BEVERAGES	

Additional Information:

So Much Fucking Wedding Attire

Hold onto your fucking hats, because it's time to dive into the world of wedding attire! From stunning gowns to dapper suits, we've got you covered.

Get ready to conquer the clothing chaos and nail that picture-perfect look.

Wedding Outfit Inspiration

Paste in all your damn
inspiration photos here!

ANOTHER FUCKING TIP: If you need a suit for your wedding day,
renting a tux can save you extra dollars. Online rental sites are a
great resource for finding a suit that fits your wedding style, budget,
and size requirements. If you're buying, take your wedding's feel into
consideration as well as its ability to be worn again for future events.

The Basics				
PIECE				
Purchased From				
Designer				
Size				
Color				
Style				
Fitting Schedule				
1st Fitting	date: time:	date: time:	date: time:	date: time:
2nd Fitting	date: time:	date: time:	date: time:	date: time:
Final Fitting	date: time:	date: time:	date: time:	date: time:
Date attire will be ready for pickup				
Picked up or delivered?				

NOTES:

The Basics				
PIECE				
Purchased From				
Designer				
Size				
Color				
Style				
Fitting Schedule				
1st Fitting	date: time:	date: time:	date: time:	date: time:
2nd Fitting	date: time:	date: time:	date: time:	date: time:
Final Fitting	date: time:	date: time:	date: time:	date: time:
Date attire will be ready for pickup				
Picked up or delivered?				

NOTES:

Keep Shit Simple: Send the Fucking Invites, Make Shit Pretty AF

Stationery			
ITEM	QUANTITY ORDERED	COST	SENT OUT/ DELIVERED

ANOTHER FUCKING TIP: Stationery is one of the easiest places to save money when it comes to your wedding budget. A quick online search can find you countless highly designed and profesh templates to print out. Even if you're not the craftiest bitch, consider trying your hand at some DIY projects with the guidance of some of the many online tutorials.

_____

_____

_____

_____

_____

_____

_____

_____

_____

_____

_____

_____

_____

_____

_____

_____

_____

_____

_____

_____

_____

ANOTHER FUCKING TIP: Decorations are a big category to tackle and can include everything from tablecloths and string lights to lanterns, candles, garlands, arches, and other unique decor items. Before buying, think about your wedding's theme, style, feel, and budget (of course). What decor items are on your must-have list? What items would you like, but could go without? Take a breath and flip back to your wedding vision at the beginning of this fucking planner to help you think through the ins and outs of your decor.

Decorations	
ITEM	COLOR/DESIGN

QUANTITY ORDERED	COST	PURCHASED/ RENTED	DELIVERED

Registry for Gifts and Other Shit

Registry Logins			
STORE	WEBSITE	LOGIN	PASSWORD

ANOTHER FUCKING TIP: Registries are a damn relief for guests since they remove the guesswork from buying gifts! When creating your registry, remember to include a variety of price points (e.g., under $50, under $75, under $150, etc.) and stores. Then, two weeks before your wedding, take a moment to update your list and add some additional items if the available inventory is low.

Registry

STORE	ITEM	QUANTITY	PRICE

Registry

STORE	ITEM	QUANTITY	PRICE

Registry

STORE	ITEM	QUANTITY	PRICE

The Big Fucking Day

When it comes to planning the big day, it's not just about throwing a bunch of shit together and hoping for the best. No, my friend, we're talking about a carefully orchestrated symphony of love, laughter, and champagne-fueled chaos. It's time to think through the order of events and get your priorities straight. Take a deep fucking breath and use this space to plan out the main events—the ceremony and the reception. This is your chance to create a damn masterpiece, a day that will be etched into the memories of your guests forever—because this is your day, your chance to say "fuck yeah" to love, commitment, and kick-ass parties.

ANOTHER FUCKING TIP: Think through the speeches and performances you will have throughout your wedding day, plus any religious, cultural, or family traditions you want to be incorporated into the events.

The Ceremony

Things to consider when planning your ceremony's order of events: the procession and the bridal/wedding party order, the officiant's remarks, special readings or music, the exchange of vows and rings, the pronouncement of marriage, the recessional, the receiving line.

The Reception

Things to consider when planning your reception's schedule: cocktail hour and pictures, introduction of the wedding party and newlyweds, first dance, champagne toast and speeches (who will be speaking?), meal, special dances, bouquet and/or garter toss, dancing, cake cutting, getaway car.

Cue the Damn Waterworks

The vows are often one of the most intimate and special parts of the entire ceremony. Whether you choose to read from a traditional script or write your own, planning your vows is a chance to reflect on what makes your relationship so fucking special!

Use these pages to think through what you want to say and include in your vows.

How did I feel about my partner when we first met? What was the moment I knew it was forever?

What do I love most about my partner and our relationship?

What makes us laugh? What makes us tick?

What do I see our future looking like?

ANOTHER FUCKING TIP: When in doubt, share a short anecdote about your relationship. Never be afraid of a little humor!

No Such Thing as Too Many Fucking Flowers

ANOTHER FUCKING TIP: Before booking flowers through a florist, find out whether your wedding/reception venue offers florist services. Working through your venue can streamline the planning process and eliminate the time spent searching for another vendor!

Flowers for:		
FLORIST		
DESCRIPTION		
DATE/TIME OF DELIVERY		COST

Flowers for:		
FLORIST		
DESCRIPTION		
DATE/TIME OF DELIVERY		COST

Flowers for:

FLORIST	
DESCRIPTION	
DATE/TIME OF DELIVERY	COST

Flowers for:

FLORIST	
DESCRIPTION	
DATE/TIME OF DELIVERY	COST

Flowers for:

FLORIST	
DESCRIPTION	
DATE/TIME OF DELIVERY	COST

Flowers for:

FLORIST	
DESCRIPTION	
DATE/TIME OF DELIVERY	COST

Flowers for the Ceremony Site

FLORIST	
DESCRIPTION	
DATE/TIME OF DELIVERY	COST

Flowers for the Ceremony Site

FLORIST	
DESCRIPTION	
DATE/TIME OF DELIVERY	COST

Flowers for the Reception

FLORIST	
DESCRIPTION	
DATE/TIME OF DELIVERY	COST

Flowers for the Reception

FLORIST	
DESCRIPTION	
DATE/TIME OF DELIVERY	COST

place a sketch or inspiration photo here

Other Decor

VENDOR	
DESCRIPTION	
DATE/TIME OF DELIVERY	COST

Badass Flower Inspiration

Paste in all your damn
inspiration photos here!

Wedding Soundtrack Is Groovy AF

The Service	
MUSICIANS/DJ	
PRELUDE & PROCESSIONAL	
CEREMONY	
RECESSIONAL	

PLAYLIST MUST-HAVES:

	Reception	
MUSICIANS/DJ		

	Musical Schedule	
#	TITLE OF SONG	MUSICIAN/BAND

ANOTHER FUCKING TIP: If you're planning a first dance, dances with the parents, or any other event needing music during the reception, use this space to think through the songs you want for each moment.

Musical Schedule

#	TITLE OF SONG	MUSICIAN/BAND

Musical Schedule		
#	TITLE OF SONG	MUSICIAN/BAND

Bitches Gotta Eat

Caterer Booked:			
FROM:		TO:	

Service Booked:			
FROM:		TO:	

Service Booked:			
FROM:		TO:	

Service Booked:			
FROM:		TO:	

Final Guest Count:		
COST PER PERSON:	# OF SERVERS:	COST PER SERVER:

MENU

HORS D'OEUVRES	
APPETIZERS	
ENTRÉES	
SIDES	
DESSERTS	
BEVERAGES	

ANOTHER FUCKING TIP: Do any of your guests have food allergies? Or is anyone vegetarian/vegan? Use this space to record any dietary restrictions that you'll need to share with your caterer.

Dietary Restrictions:

place a sketch or inspiration photo here

The Cake/Dessert

BAKER NAME	
BAKER CONTACT INFO	
NUMBER OF SLICES	
COST	
DESCRIPTION	
OTHER	

ANOTHER FUCKING TIP: Other things to consider when ordering your wedding cake or dessert are toppers, display stands, serving sets, and to-go boxes for guests to take slices home.

When the Party's Fucking Over

After-Wedding Checklist		
TASK	DUE BY	DONE

ANOTHER FUCKING TIP: The to-do list doesn't end once your wedding is over. As you go through the planning, write down the due dates for rented items, vendor payments, and sending thank-you notes. Then make sure you get it fucking done!

TASK	DUE BY	DONE

Fuck Yeah! Honeymoon!

- [ ] Decide on a location.

- [ ] Book transportation (e.g., flight reservations, rental cars, train tickets, cruise ship reservations.)

- [ ] Reserve hotel room or vacation rental.

- [ ] Schedule your activities (e.g., spa reservations, food tours, wine tastings, private boat tours, etc.)

- [ ] Start packing the essentials (e.g., passports, credit cards, reservation confirmations, passport/ID photocopies, etc.)

- [ ] Pack clothes, toiletries, and accessories for your activities.

ANOTHER FUCKING TIP: Your honeymoon doesn't have to include sun and surf. Choose a destination that you and your partner will both enjoy, fits your budget constraints, and has the weather you're looking for!

MONTH & YEAR: _____

sunday	monday	tuesday	wednesday	thursday	friday	saturday

badass bride to be

● monday

Morning

Afternoon

Night

● tuesday

Morning

Afternoon

Night

● wednesday

Morning

Afternoon

Night

General Shit to Do

Wedding Shit to Do

● thursday

Morning

Afternoon

Night

● friday

Morning

Afternoon

Night

● saturday

Morning

Afternoon

Night

● sunday

Morning

Afternoon

Night

Self-Fucking-Care

FOR ME

FOR US

___ / ___ / ___ to ___ / ___ / ___

● monday

Morning

Afternoon

Night

● tuesday

Morning

Afternoon

Night

● wednesday

Morning

Afternoon

Night

General Shit to Do

Wedding Shit to Do

● thursday

Morning

Afternoon

Night

● friday

Morning

Afternoon

Night

● saturday

Morning

Afternoon

Night

● sunday

Morning

Afternoon

Night

Self-Fucking-Care

FOR ME

_____

_____

_____

_____

FOR US

_____

_____

_____

_____

● monday

Morning

Afternoon

Night

● tuesday

Morning

Afternoon

Night

● wednesday

Morning

Afternoon

Night

General Shit to Do

Wedding Shit to Do

thursday

Morning

Afternoon

Night

friday

Morning

Afternoon

Night

saturday

Morning

Afternoon

Night

sunday

Morning

Afternoon

Night

Self-Fucking-Care

FOR ME

FOR US

● monday

Morning

Afternoon

Night

● tuesday

Morning

Afternoon

Night

● wednesday

Morning

Afternoon

Night

General Shit to Do

Wedding Shit to Do

● thursday

Morning

Afternoon

Night

● friday

Morning

Afternoon

Night

● saturday

Morning

Afternoon

Night

● sunday

Morning

Afternoon

Night

Self-Fucking-Care

FOR ME

FOR US

___ / ___ / ___ to ___ / ___ / ___

● monday

Morning

Afternoon

Night

● tuesday

Morning

Afternoon

Night

● wednesday

Morning

Afternoon

Night

General Shit to Do

Wedding Shit to Do

● thursday

Morning

Afternoon

Night

● friday

Morning

Afternoon

Night

● saturday

Morning

Afternoon

Night

● sunday

Morning

Afternoon

Night

Self-Fucking-Care

FOR ME

FOR US

MONTH & YEAR: _____

sunday	monday	tuesday	wednesday	thursday	friday	saturday

look at you!
getting all engaged & shit

___ / ___ / ___ to ___ / ___ / ___

● monday

Morning

Afternoon

Night

● tuesday

Morning

Afternoon

Night

● wednesday

Morning

Afternoon

Night

General Shit to Do

Wedding Shit to Do

thursday

Morning

Afternoon

Night

friday

Morning

Afternoon

Night

saturday

Morning

Afternoon

Night

sunday

Morning

Afternoon

Night

Self-Fucking-Care

FOR ME

FOR US

___ /___ /___ to ___ /___ /___

● monday

Morning

Afternoon

Night

● tuesday

Morning

Afternoon

Night

● wednesday

Morning

Afternoon

Night

General Shit to Do

Wedding Shit to Do

● thursday

Morning

Afternoon

Night

● friday

Morning

Afternoon

Night

● saturday

Morning

Afternoon

Night

● sunday

Morning

Afternoon

Night

Self-Fucking-Care

FOR ME	FOR US

● monday

Morning

Afternoon

Night

● tuesday

Morning

Afternoon

Night

● wednesday

Morning

Afternoon

Night

General Shit to Do

Wedding Shit to Do

● thursday

Morning

Afternoon

Night

● friday

Morning

Afternoon

Night

● saturday

Morning

Afternoon

Night

● sunday

Morning

Afternoon

Night

Self-Fucking-Care

FOR ME

FOR US

___ /___ /___ to ___ /___ /___

● monday

Morning

Afternoon

Night

● tuesday

Morning

Afternoon

Night

● wednesday

Morning

Afternoon

Night

General Shit to Do

Wedding Shit to Do

● thursday

Morning

Afternoon

Night

● friday

Morning

Afternoon

Night

● saturday

Morning

Afternoon

Night

● sunday

Morning

Afternoon

Night

Self-Fucking-Care

FOR ME

FOR US

MONTH & YEAR: _____

sunday	monday	tuesday	wednesday	thursday	friday	saturday

___ /___ /___ to ___ /___ /___

● monday

Morning

Afternoon

Night

● tuesday

Morning

Afternoon

Night

● wednesday

Morning

Afternoon

Night

General Shit to Do

Wedding Shit to Do

● thursday

Morning

Afternoon

Night

● friday

Morning

Afternoon

Night

● saturday

Morning

Afternoon

Night

● sunday

Morning

Afternoon

Night

Self-Fucking-Care

FOR ME

FOR US

___ / ___ / ___ to ___ / ___ / ___

● monday

Morning

Afternoon

Night

● tuesday

Morning

Afternoon

Night

● wednesday

Morning

Afternoon

Night

General Shit to Do

Wedding Shit to Do

● thursday

Morning

Afternoon

Night

● friday

Morning

Afternoon

Night

● saturday

Morning

Afternoon

Night

● sunday

Morning

Afternoon

Night

Self-Fucking-Care

FOR ME	FOR US

___ /___ /___ to ___ /___ /___

● monday

Morning

Afternoon

Night

● tuesday

Morning

Afternoon

Night

● wednesday

Morning

Afternoon

Night

General Shit to Do

Wedding Shit to Do

🔘 thursday

Morning

Afternoon

Night

🔘 friday

Morning

Afternoon

Night

🔘 saturday

Morning

Afternoon

Night

🔘 sunday

Morning

Afternoon

Night

Self-Fucking-Care

FOR ME

FOR US

monday

Morning

Afternoon

Night

tuesday

Morning

Afternoon

Night

wednesday

Morning

Afternoon

Night

General Shit to Do

Wedding Shit to Do

● thursday

Morning

Afternoon

Night

● friday

Morning

Afternoon

Night

● saturday

Morning

Afternoon

Night

● sunday

Morning

Afternoon

Night

Self-Fucking-Care

FOR ME

FOR US

___ /___ /___ to ___ /___ /___

monday

Morning

Afternoon

Night

tuesday

Morning

Afternoon

Night

wednesday

Morning

Afternoon

Night

General Shit to Do

Wedding Shit to Do

thursday

Morning

Afternoon

Night

friday

Morning

Afternoon

Night

saturday

Morning

Afternoon

Night

sunday

Morning

Afternoon

Night

Self-Fucking-Care

FOR ME

FOR US

MONTH & YEAR: _____

sunday	monday	tuesday	wednesday	thursday	friday	saturday

biggest
day of your
fucking life

(no pressure)

___ / ___ / ___ to ___ / ___ / ___

● monday

Morning

Afternoon

Night

● tuesday

Morning

Afternoon

Night

● wednesday

Morning

Afternoon

Night

General Shit to Do

Wedding Shit to Do

● thursday

Morning

Afternoon

Night

● friday

Morning

Afternoon

Night

● saturday

Morning

Afternoon

Night

● sunday

Morning

Afternoon

Night

Self-Fucking-Care

FOR ME

_____

_____

_____

_____

FOR US

_____

_____

_____

_____

___ /___ /___ to ___ /___ /___

monday

Morning

Afternoon

Night

tuesday

Morning

Afternoon

Night

wednesday

Morning

Afternoon

Night

General Shit to Do

Wedding Shit to Do

● thursday

Morning

Afternoon

Night

● friday

Morning

Afternoon

Night

● saturday

Morning

Afternoon

Night

● sunday

Morning

Afternoon

Night

Self-Fucking-Care

FOR ME

FOR US

___ / ___ / ___ to ___ / ___ / ___

● monday

Morning

Afternoon

Night

● tuesday

Morning

Afternoon

Night

● wednesday

Morning

Afternoon

Night

General Shit to Do

Wedding Shit to Do

● thursday

Morning

Afternoon

Night

● friday

Morning

Afternoon

Night

● saturday

Morning

Afternoon

Night

● sunday

Morning

Afternoon

Night

Self-Fucking-Care

FOR ME

FOR US

___ /___ /___ to ___ /___ /___

● monday

Morning

Afternoon

Night

● tuesday

Morning

Afternoon

Night

● wednesday

Morning

Afternoon

Night

General Shit to Do

Wedding Shit to Do

thursday

Morning

Afternoon

Night

friday

Morning

Afternoon

Night

saturday

Morning

Afternoon

Night

sunday

Morning

Afternoon

Night

Self-Fucking-Care

FOR ME	FOR US

MONTH & YEAR: _____

sunday	monday	tuesday	wednesday	thursday	friday	saturday

☑ **wake up,**

☑ **make some damn wedding plans,**

☑ *repeat*

___ /___ /___ to ___ /___ /___

● **monday**

Morning

Afternoon

Night

● **tuesday**

Morning

Afternoon

Night

● **wednesday**

Morning

Afternoon

Night

General Shit to Do

Wedding Shit to Do

● thursday

Morning

Afternoon

Night

● friday

Morning

Afternoon

Night

● saturday

Morning

Afternoon

Night

● sunday

Morning

Afternoon

Night

Self-Fucking-Care

FOR ME

FOR US

● monday

Morning

Afternoon

Night

● tuesday

Morning

Afternoon

Night

● wednesday

Morning

Afternoon

Night

General Shit to Do

Wedding Shit to Do

● thursday

Morning

Afternoon

Night

● friday

Morning

Afternoon

Night

● saturday

Morning

Afternoon

Night

● sunday

Morning

Afternoon

Night

Self-Fucking-Care

FOR ME

FOR US

___ /___ /___ to ___ /___ /___

● monday

Morning

Afternoon

Night

● tuesday

Morning

Afternoon

Night

● wednesday

Morning

Afternoon

Night

General Shit to Do

Wedding Shit to Do

⬤ thursday

Morning

Afternoon

Night

⬤ friday

Morning

Afternoon

Night

⬤ saturday

Morning

Afternoon

Night

⬤ sunday

Morning

Afternoon

Night

Self-Fucking-Care

FOR ME

FOR US

● monday

Morning

Afternoon

Night

● tuesday

Morning

Afternoon

Night

● wednesday

Morning

Afternoon

Night

General Shit to Do

Wedding Shit to Do

● thursday

Morning

Afternoon

Night

● friday

Morning

Afternoon

Night

● saturday

Morning

Afternoon

Night

● sunday

Morning

Afternoon

Night

Self-Fucking-Care

FOR ME

FOR US

____ / ____ / ____ to ____ / ____ / ____

● monday

Morning

Afternoon

Night

● tuesday

Morning

Afternoon

Night

● wednesday

Morning

Afternoon

Night

General Shit to Do

Wedding Shit to Do

144

● thursday

Morning

Afternoon

Night

● friday

Morning

Afternoon

Night

● saturday

Morning

Afternoon

Night

● sunday

Morning

Afternoon

Night

Self-Fucking-Care

FOR ME

FOR US

MONTH & YEAR: _____

sunday	monday	tuesday	wednesday	thursday	friday	saturday

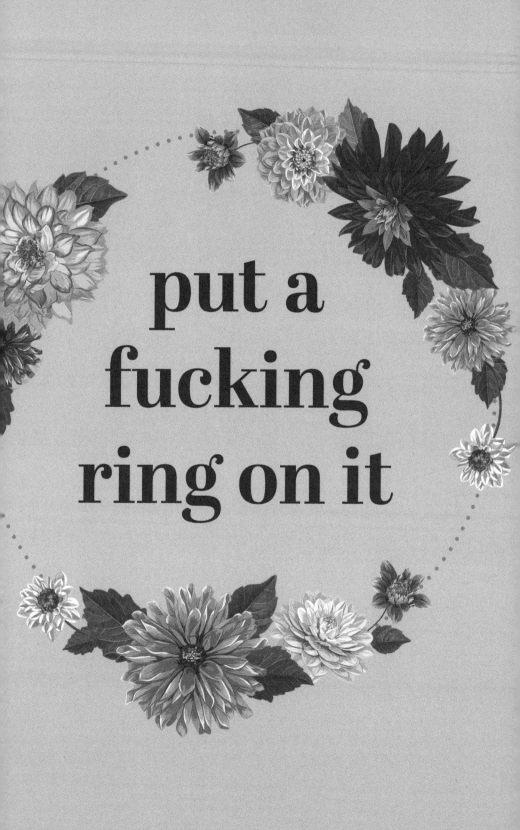

put a
fucking
ring on it

● monday

Morning

Afternoon

Night

● tuesday

Morning

Afternoon

Night

● wednesday

Morning

Afternoon

Night

General Shit to Do

Wedding Shit to Do

● thursday

Morning

Afternoon

Night

● friday

Morning

Afternoon

Night

● saturday

Morning

Afternoon

Night

● sunday

Morning

Afternoon

Night

Self-Fucking-Care

FOR ME

FOR US

____ / ____ / ____ to ____ / ____ / ____

● monday

Morning

Afternoon

Night

● tuesday

Morning

Afternoon

Night

● wednesday

Morning

Afternoon

Night

General Shit to Do

Wedding Shit to Do

● thursday

Morning

Afternoon

Night

● friday

Morning

Afternoon

Night

● saturday

Morning

Afternoon

Night

● sunday

Morning

Afternoon

Night

Self-Fucking-Care

FOR ME

FOR US

monday

Morning

Afternoon

Night

tuesday

Morning

Afternoon

Night

wednesday

Morning

Afternoon

Night

General Shit to Do

Wedding Shit to Do

● thursday

Morning

Afternoon

Night

● friday

Morning

Afternoon

Night

● saturday

Morning

Afternoon

Night

● sunday

Morning

Afternoon

Night

Self-Fucking-Care

FOR ME

FOR US

___ /___ /___ to ___ /___ /___

monday

Morning

Afternoon

Night

tuesday

Morning

Afternoon

Night

wednesday

Morning

Afternoon

Night

General Shit to Do

Wedding Shit to Do

thursday

Morning

Afternoon

Night

friday

Morning

Afternoon

Night

saturday

Morning

Afternoon

Night

sunday

Morning

Afternoon

Night

Self-Fucking-Care

FOR ME

FOR US

MONTH & YEAR: _____

sunday	monday	tuesday	wednesday	thursday	friday	saturday

bitches better
RSVP

● monday

Morning

Afternoon

Night

● tuesday

Morning

Afternoon

Night

● wednesday

Morning

Afternoon

Night

General Shit to Do

Wedding Shit to Do

● thursday

Morning

Afternoon

Night

● friday

Morning

Afternoon

Night

● saturday

Morning

Afternoon

Night

● sunday

Morning

Afternoon

Night

Self-Fucking-Care

FOR ME

FOR US

___ /___ /___ to ___ /___ /___

● monday

Morning

Afternoon

Night

● tuesday

Morning

Afternoon

Night

● wednesday

Morning

Afternoon

Night

General Shit to Do

Wedding Shit to Do

● thursday

Morning

Afternoon

Night

● friday

Morning

Afternoon

Night

● saturday

Morning

Afternoon

Night

● sunday

Morning

Afternoon

Night

Self-Fucking-Care

FOR ME	FOR US

___ / ___ / ___ to ___ / ___ / ___

● monday

Morning

Afternoon

Night

● tuesday

Morning

Afternoon

Night

● wednesday

Morning

Afternoon

Night

General Shit to Do

Wedding Shit to Do

● thursday

Morning

Afternoon

Night

● friday

Morning

Afternoon

Night

● saturday

Morning

Afternoon

Night

● sunday

Morning

Afternoon

Night

Self-Fucking-Care

FOR ME

FOR US

___ / ___ / ___ to ___ / ___ / ___

● monday

Morning

Afternoon

Night

● tuesday

Morning

Afternoon

Night

● wednesday

Morning

Afternoon

Night

General Shit to Do

Wedding Shit to Do

● thursday

Morning

Afternoon

Night

● friday

Morning

Afternoon

Night

● saturday

Morning

Afternoon

Night

● sunday

Morning

Afternoon

Night

Self-Fucking-Care

FOR ME

FOR US

___ /___ /___ to ___ /___ /___

monday

Morning

Afternoon

Night

tuesday

Morning

Afternoon

Night

wednesday

Morning

Afternoon

Night

General Shit to Do

Wedding Shit to Do

● thursday

Morning

Afternoon

Night

● friday

Morning

Afternoon

Night

● saturday

Morning

Afternoon

Night

● sunday

Morning

Afternoon

Night

Self-Fucking-Care

FOR ME

FOR US

MONTH & YEAR: _____

sunday	monday	tuesday	wednesday	thursday	friday	saturday

eat,
drink,
and be
married
AF

___ / ___ / ___ to ___ / ___ / ___

● monday

Morning

Afternoon

Night

● tuesday

Morning

Afternoon

Night

● wednesday

Morning

Afternoon

Night

General Shit to Do

Wedding Shit to Do

● thursday

Morning

Afternoon

Night

● friday

Morning

Afternoon

Night

● saturday

Morning

Afternoon

Night

● sunday

Morning

Afternoon

Night

Self-Fucking-Care

FOR ME	FOR US

monday

Morning

Afternoon

Night

tuesday

Morning

Afternoon

Night

wednesday

Morning

Afternoon

Night

General Shit to Do

Wedding Shit to Do

● thursday

Morning

Afternoon

Night

● friday

Morning

Afternoon

Night

● saturday

Morning

Afternoon

Night

● sunday

Morning

Afternoon

Night

Self-Fucking-Care

FOR ME

FOR US

___ /___ /___ to ___ /___ /___

monday

Morning

Afternoon

Night

tuesday

Morning

Afternoon

Night

wednesday

Morning

Afternoon

Night

General Shit to Do

Wedding Shit to Do

● thursday

Morning

Afternoon

Night

● friday

Morning

Afternoon

Night

● saturday

Morning

Afternoon

Night

● sunday

Morning

Afternoon

Night

Self-Fucking-Care

FOR ME

FOR US

___ /___ /___ to ___ /___ /___

● monday

Morning

Afternoon

Night

● tuesday

Morning

Afternoon

Night

● wednesday

Morning

Afternoon

Night

General Shit to Do

Wedding Shit to Do

🔘 thursday

Morning

Afternoon

Night

🔘 friday

Morning

Afternoon

Night

🔘 saturday

Morning

Afternoon

Night

🔘 sunday

Morning

Afternoon

Night

Self-Fucking-Care

FOR ME

FOR US

MONTH & YEAR: _____

sunday	monday	tuesday	wednesday	thursday	friday	saturday

about.
damn.
time.

___ / ___ / ___ to ___ / ___ / ___

● monday

Morning

Afternoon

Night

● tuesday

Morning

Afternoon

Night

● wednesday

Morning

Afternoon

Night

General Shit to Do

Wedding Shit to Do

● thursday

Morning

Afternoon

Night

● friday

Morning

Afternoon

Night

● saturday

Morning

Afternoon

Night

● sunday

Morning

Afternoon

Night

Self-Fucking-Care

FOR ME

FOR US

monday

Morning
Afternoon
Night

tuesday

Morning
Afternoon
Night

wednesday

Morning
Afternoon
Night

General Shit to Do

_____

_____

_____

_____

Wedding Shit to Do

_____

_____

_____

_____

● thursday

Morning

Afternoon

Night

● friday

Morning

Afternoon

Night

● saturday

Morning

Afternoon

Night

● sunday

Morning

Afternoon

Night

Self-Fucking-Care

FOR ME	FOR US

___ / ___ / ___ to ___ / ___ / ___

● monday

Morning

Afternoon

Night

● tuesday

Morning

Afternoon

Night

● wednesday

Morning

Afternoon

Night

General Shit to Do

Wedding Shit to Do

● thursday

Morning

Afternoon

Night

● friday

Morning

Afternoon

Night

● saturday

Morning

Afternoon

Night

● sunday

Morning

Afternoon

Night

Self-Fucking-Care

FOR ME

FOR US

___ /___ /___ to ___ /___ /___

● monday

Morning

Afternoon

Night

● tuesday

Morning

Afternoon

Night

● wednesday

Morning

Afternoon

Night

General Shit to Do

Wedding Shit to Do

● thursday

Morning

Afternoon

Night

● friday

Morning

Afternoon

Night

● saturday

Morning

Afternoon

Night

● sunday

Morning

Afternoon

Night

Self-Fucking-Care

FOR ME

FOR US

___ /___ /___ to ___ /___ /___

● monday

Morning

Afternoon

Night

● tuesday

Morning

Afternoon

Night

● wednesday

Morning

Afternoon

Night

General Shit to Do

Wedding Shit to Do

● thursday

Morning

Afternoon

Night

● friday

Morning

Afternoon

Night

● saturday

Morning

Afternoon

Night

● sunday

Morning

Afternoon

Night

Self-Fucking-Care

FOR ME

FOR US

MONTH & YEAR: _____

sunday	monday	tuesday	wednesday	thursday	friday	saturday

shit's about to get real

___ /___ /___ to ___ /___ /___

monday

Morning

Afternoon

Night

tuesday

Morning

Afternoon

Night

wednesday

Morning

Afternoon

Night

General Shit to Do

Wedding Shit to Do

● thursday

Morning

Afternoon

Night

● friday

Morning

Afternoon

Night

● saturday

Morning

Afternoon

Night

● sunday

Morning

Afternoon

Night

Self-Fucking-Care

FOR ME

FOR US

● monday

Morning

Afternoon

Night

● tuesday

Morning

Afternoon

Night

● wednesday

Morning

Afternoon

Night

General Shit to Do

Wedding Shit to Do

● thursday

Morning

Afternoon

Night

● friday

Morning

Afternoon

Night

● saturday

Morning

Afternoon

Night

● sunday

Morning

Afternoon

Night

Self-Fucking-Care

FOR ME

FOR US

___ /___ /___ to ___ /___ /___

monday

Morning

Afternoon

Night

tuesday

Morning

Afternoon

Night

wednesday

Morning

Afternoon

Night

General Shit to Do

Wedding Shit to Do

● thursday

Morning

Afternoon

Night

● friday

Morning

Afternoon

Night

● saturday

Morning

Afternoon

Night

● sunday

Morning

Afternoon

Night

Self-Fucking-Care

FOR ME

FOR US

___ / ___ / ___ to ___ / ___ / ___

monday

Morning

Afternoon

Night

tuesday

Morning

Afternoon

Night

wednesday

Morning

Afternoon

Night

General Shit to Do

Wedding Shit to Do

● thursday

Morning

Afternoon

Night

● friday

Morning

Afternoon

Night

● saturday

Morning

Afternoon

Night

● sunday

Morning

Afternoon

Night

Self-Fucking-Care

FOR ME

FOR US

MONTH & YEAR: _____

sunday	monday	tuesday	wednesday	thursday	friday	saturday

planning
that
happily
ever
fucking
after

● monday

Morning

Afternoon

Night

● tuesday

Morning

Afternoon

Night

● wednesday

Morning

Afternoon

Night

General Shit to Do

Wedding Shit to Do

● thursday

Morning

Afternoon

Night

● friday

Morning

Afternoon

Night

● saturday

Morning

Afternoon

Night

● sunday

Morning

Afternoon

Night

Self-Fucking-Care

FOR ME

FOR US

● monday

Morning

Afternoon

Night

● tuesday

Morning

Afternoon

Night

● wednesday

Morning

Afternoon

Night

General Shit to Do

Wedding Shit to Do

● thursday

Morning

Afternoon

Night

● friday

Morning

Afternoon

Night

● saturday

Morning

Afternoon

Night

● sunday

Morning

Afternoon

Night

Self-Fucking-Care

FOR ME

FOR US

● monday

Morning

Afternoon

Night

● tuesday

Morning

Afternoon

Night

● wednesday

Morning

Afternoon

Night

General Shit to Do

Wedding Shit to Do

● thursday

Morning

Afternoon

Night

● friday

Morning

Afternoon

Night

● saturday

Morning

Afternoon

Night

● sunday

Morning

Afternoon

Night

Self-Fucking-Care

FOR ME

FOR US

● monday

Morning

Afternoon

Night

● tuesday

Morning

Afternoon

Night

● wednesday

Morning

Afternoon

Night

General Shit to Do

Wedding Shit to Do

● thursday

Morning

Afternoon

Night

● friday

Morning

Afternoon

Night

● saturday

Morning

Afternoon

Night

● sunday

Morning

Afternoon

Night

Self-Fucking-Care

FOR ME

FOR US

___ /___ /___ to ___ /___ /___

● monday

Morning

Afternoon

Night

● tuesday

Morning

Afternoon

Night

● wednesday

Morning

Afternoon

Night

General Shit to Do

Wedding Shit to Do

● thursday

Morning

Afternoon

Night

● friday

Morning

Afternoon

Night

● saturday

Morning

Afternoon

Night

● sunday

Morning

Afternoon

Night

Self-Fucking-Care

FOR ME

FOR US

MONTH & YEAR: _____

sunday	monday	tuesday	wednesday	thursday	friday	saturday

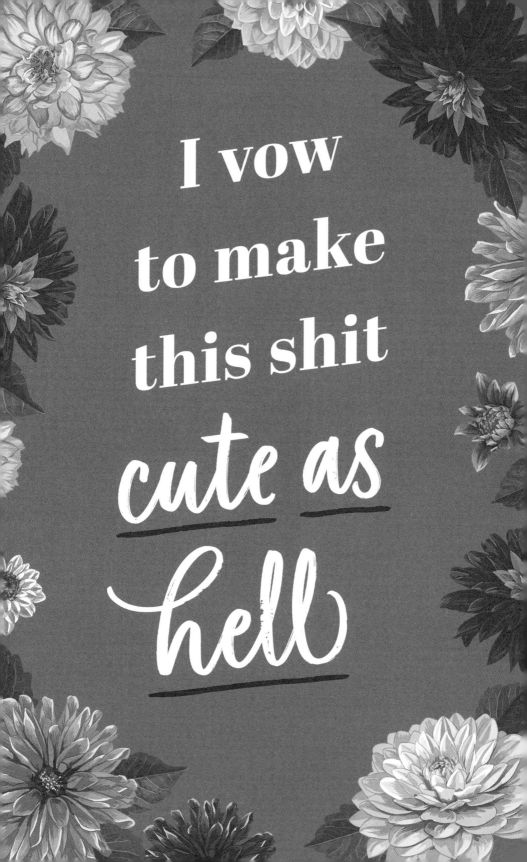

___ /___ /___ to ___ /___ /___

monday

Morning

Afternoon

Night

tuesday

Morning

Afternoon

Night

wednesday

Morning

Afternoon

Night

General Shit to Do

Wedding Shit to Do

● thursday

Morning

Afternoon

Night

● friday

Morning

Afternoon

Night

● saturday

Morning

Afternoon

Night

● sunday

Morning

Afternoon

Night

Self-Fucking-Care

FOR ME

FOR US

___ /___ /___ to ___ /___ /___

● monday

Morning

Afternoon

Night

● tuesday

Morning

Afternoon

Night

● wednesday

Morning

Afternoon

Night

General Shit to Do

Wedding Shit to Do

🔘 thursday

Morning

Afternoon

Night

🔘 friday

Morning

Afternoon

Night

🔘 saturday

Morning

Afternoon

Night

🔘 sunday

Morning

Afternoon

Night

Self-Fucking-Care

FOR ME

_____

_____

_____

_____

FOR US

_____

_____

_____

_____

● monday

Morning

Afternoon

Night

● tuesday

Morning

Afternoon

Night

● wednesday

Morning

Afternoon

Night

General Shit to Do

Wedding Shit to Do

● thursday

Morning

Afternoon

Night

● friday

Morning

Afternoon

Night

● saturday

Morning

Afternoon

Night

● sunday

Morning

Afternoon

Night

Self-Fucking-Care

FOR ME

FOR US

● monday

Morning

Afternoon

Night

● tuesday

Morning

Afternoon

Night

● wednesday

Morning

Afternoon

Night

General Shit to Do

Wedding Shit to Do

● thursday

Morning

Afternoon

Night

● friday

Morning

Afternoon

Night

● saturday

Morning

Afternoon

Night

● sunday

Morning

Afternoon

Night

Self-Fucking-Care

FOR ME

FOR US

Published by Sourcebooks
P.O. Box 4410, Naperville, Illinois 60567-4410
(630) 961-3900
sourcebooks.com

Printed and bound in China.
OGP 10 9 8 7 6 5 4 3 2 1

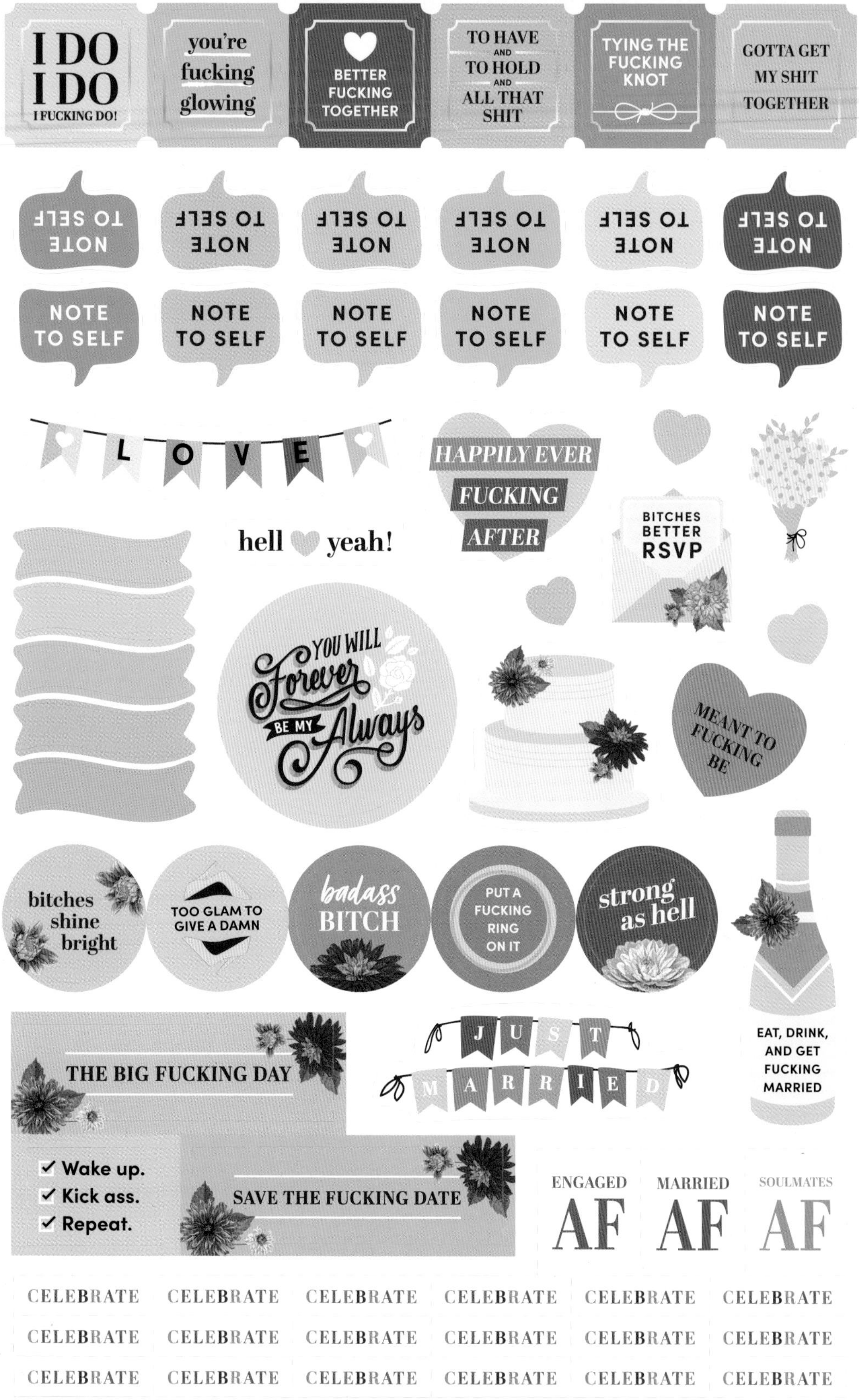

I DO I DO I FUCKING DO!
you're fucking glowing
BETTER FUCKING TOGETHER
TO HAVE AND TO HOLD AND ALL THAT SHIT
TYING THE FUCKING KNOT
GOTTA GET MY SHIT TOGETHER
NOTE TO SELF
NOTE TO SELF
NOTE TO SELF
NOTE TO SELF
NOTE TO SELF
NOTE TO SELF
NOTE TO SELF
NOTE TO SELF
NOTE TO SELF
NOTE TO SELF
NOTE TO SELF
NOTE TO SELF
LOVE
HAPPILY EVER FUCKING AFTER
hell yeah!
BITCHES BETTER RSVP
YOU WILL BE MY Forever Always
MEANT TO FUCKING BE
bitches shine bright
TOO GLAM TO GIVE A DAMN
badass BITCH
PUT A FUCKING RING ON IT
strong as hell
EAT, DRINK, AND GET FUCKING MARRIED
THE BIG FUCKING DAY
JUST MARRIED
Wake up.
Kick ass.
Repeat.
SAVE THE FUCKING DATE
ENGAGED AF
MARRIED AF
SOULMATES AF
CELEBRATE
CELEBRATE
CELEBRATE
CELEBRATE
CELEBRATE
CELEBRATE
CELEBRATE
CELEBRATE
CELEBRATE
CELEBRATE
CELEBRATE
CELEBRATE
CELEBRATE
CELEBRATE
CELEBRATE
CELEBRATE
CELEBRATE
CELEBRATE

| SELF-CARE | SELF-CARE | SELF-CARE | SELF-CARE | SELF-CARE | SELF-CARE |
| SELF-CARE | SELF-CARE | SELF-CARE | SELF-CARE | SELF-CARE | SELF-CARE |

| PLANS | PLANS | PLANS | PLANS | PLANS | PLANS |
| PLANS | PLANS | PLANS | PLANS | PLANS | PLANS |

| vacation | vacation | vacation | vacation | vacation | vacation |
| vacation | vacation | vacation | vacation | vacation | vacation |

appointment	appointment	appointment	appointment	appointment	appointment
appointment	appointment	appointment	appointment	appointment	appointment
appointment	appointment	appointment	appointment	appointment	appointment

| reset | refresh | reset | refresh | reset | refresh |
| refresh | reset | refresh | reset | refresh | reset |

| TO DO | TO DO | TO DO | TO DO | TO DO | TO DO |
| TO DO | TO DO | TO DO | TO DO | TO DO | TO DO |

MEETING	MEETING	MEETING	MEETING	MEETING	MEETING
MEETING	MEETING	MEETING	MEETING	MEETING	MEETING
MEETING	MEETING	MEETING	MEETING	MEETING	MEETING

| goals | goals | goals | goals | goals | goals |
| goals | goals | goals | goals | goals | goals |

| Important! | Important! | Important! | Important! | Important! | Important! |
| Important! | Important! | Important! | Important! | Important! | Important! |

BILLS DUE	BILLS DUE	BILLS DUE	BILLS DUE	BILLS DUE	BILLS DUE
BILLS DUE	BILLS DUE	BILLS DUE	BILLS DUE	BILLS DUE	BILLS DUE
BILLS DUE	BILLS DUE	BILLS DUE	BILLS DUE	BILLS DUE	BILLS DUE
BILLS DUE	BILLS DUE	BILLS DUE	BILLS DUE	BILLS DUE	BILLS DUE
BILLS DUE	BILLS DUE	BILLS DUE	BILLS DUE	BILLS DUE	BILLS DUE

PAYDAY	PAYDAY	PAYDAY	PAYDAY	PAYDAY	PAYDAY
PAYDAY	PAYDAY	PAYDAY	PAYDAY	PAYDAY	PAYDAY
PAYDAY	PAYDAY	PAYDAY	PAYDAY	PAYDAY	PAYDAY
PAYDAY	PAYDAY	PAYDAY	PAYDAY	PAYDAY	PAYDAY
PAYDAY	PAYDAY	PAYDAY	PAYDAY	PAYDAY	PAYDAY